CONTENTS

Shopping across the generations at the Reminiscence Centre.

1 ABOUT AGE EXCHANGE

REMINISCENCE THEATRE

Age Exchange runs a professional theatre company which presents plays based on older people's memories to audiences of all ages, but especially to older people in residential settings. These plays are presented all over Britain, and increasingly in European countries.

REMINISCENCE CENTRE

Its base is the Reminiscence Centre in South East London, a unique community centre for older people where there are a variety of reminiscence activities, many of them involving younger people.

HANDS - ON MUSEUM AND GALLERY

There is a permanent collection of everyday objects from the 1920s and 30s which can be handled by visitors of all ages, and three or four exhibitions each year on reminiscence themes in the gallery space.

EDUCATIONAL THEATRE PROJECTS

Many of these three-dimensional exhibitions have also served as the set or environment for Theatre in Education projects for school children. Professional actors and older people explore reminiscence themes with children through drama and theatre over a whole day at the Reminiscence Centre.

EDUCATIONAL RESOURCES

Age Exchange have developed a number of Reminiscence Boxes which can be hired by schools or by older people's groups. Objects, images and artifacts around a theme such as schooldays or housework (and ideas on how to use them) provide material for the exchange of stories and activities between young and old.

PROFESSIONAL TRAINING PROGRAMMES

There are also training courses in reminiscence for professionals working with older people and for teachers wishing to introduce reminiscence and oral history into their teaching programmes. About forty of these courses are run each year from the Centre, but others take place in different training centres all over the country.

Age Exchange is a voluntary organisation and a registered charity. Its aim is to improve the quality of life of older people by emphasising the value of their reminiscences to young and old through educational and artistic activities.

Children listening to older people's stories of the war years in the Age Exchange Reminiscence Centre.

2 A DECADE OF INTER-GENERATIONAL INITIATIVES BY AGE EXCHANGE

Since 1983, Age Exchange has been actively promoting projects which involve older people and schoolchildren working together. Some of the projects have been very modest small-scale operations involving two or three meetings between a single class of children and one or two older people. Others have been highly ambitious, involving the creation of special 3-D environments and a complete participatory play for children and older people by a professional acting company.

In fact it will be clear from the descriptions of these projects that the smallest of them is capable of all manner of extensions, and that the most ambitious programmes described can be replicated on a more economical scale at classroom level by the imaginative teacher. Some projects have involved working with class teachers within the school curriculum, and more recently within the National Curriculum. Others have been extra-mural activities pursued by children with older people in their own time,

often through the Age Exchange Reminiscence Centre or outreach projects set up by Age Exchange in other parts of the country.

The intention behind recording these projects is to stimulate ideas and initiatives involving children and older people in schools and in the wider community. This publication marks the tenth anniversary of Age Exchange and the European Year of Older People and Solidarity Between Generations.

PRIMARY AND SECONDARY LEVELS

The examples provided are intended to demonstrate the range of approaches available to those wishing to work through reminiscence and oral history across the generations in both primary and secondary schools. Suggestions are offered as to how the activities described relate to different areas of the National Curriculum, but all of the ideas can be adapted to different levels and attainment targets depending on the age and circumstances of the children.

Joan Pearce tells children stories about how she was evacuated when she was their age.

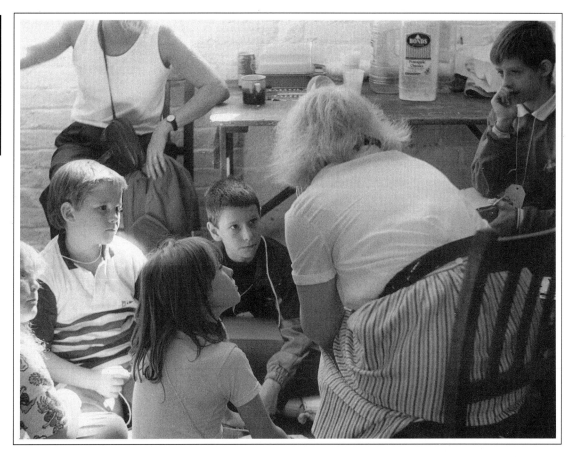

3 WHY START INTER-GENERATIONAL REMINISCENCE WORK?

'This is how it was.' An age exchange in Maerdy in the Rhondda Valley, Wales.

Underlying all of these programmes of work has been a desire to create good relationships between children and older people growing out of joint creative activity. Giving classroom time to inter-generational reminiscence work puts a high value on the life experience of older people, encouraging young people to listen to what they have to say and to use the new knowledge in their work. It increases the sense of community of both groups and can considerably improve their quality of life.

An observer recently attended an inter-generational reminiscence session based in a primary school in which two older people from the Age Exchange Reminiscence Centre unpacked a Reminiscence Box (see section later) on school days and reflected with the children on the contents. He noted the following **REWARDS** for the children and the older people:

REWARDS FOR THE CHILDREN:

■ A change in the routine
■ An air of excitement and expectancy
■ Meeting new people in the classroom
■ First-hand presentation of information/experience
■ Associating the past with real living people
■ Understanding some of the ways in which things have changed
■ Being able to imagine what the older people's childhood was like
■ Testing their beliefs/preconceptions with the older people
■ Discovering new information
■ Positive reinforcement of curiosity
■ Being able to demonstrate their own knowledge
■ Applying new information to their own family (especially grandparents)
■ Handling and experimenting with unfamiliar objects
■ Sharing objects with classmates
■ Demonstrating newly-learned skills
■ Acting out ideas about the past
■ Dressing up and fantasy work
■ Enjoyment of humour of old schooldays stories
■ Surprise, even astonishment, in stories (especially over punishments)
■ Increasing vocabulary
■ Being treated respectfully by a respected older person
■ Appreciation of modern opportunities
■ Increased consciousness of their own educational processes

REWARDS FOR THE OLDER PEOPLE:

- Meeting and working alongside teachers
- Recalling their own schooldays in the school setting
- Noticing continuities and changes in the school environment
- Seeing the common threads between generations of children
- Being appreciated for one's special life experience
- Gaining the attention of a younger age group
- Realising the depth of one's own knowledge
- Passing on skills and knowledge
- Sharing personal information in a friendly atmosphere
- Enjoying the enthusiasm and playfulness of the children
- Being able to satisfy a child's thirst for knowledge
- Remembering the simple pleasures of one's own childhood
- Knowing that one's own past is of present-day interest
- Seeing the children's expressions of fascination and discovery
- Answering questions with growing confidence
- Enlarging upon any issues arising
- Ensuring everyone is involved
- Providing stimulating resources for classroom use
- Being thanked and appreciated by children and teachers

Jim Hughes demonstrates the delights of the gas mask to Primary school children.

Emma Dean, a Somerset pupil, comments on her experience of making a play from older people's memories.

It kept us going   Emma Dean

It started as fun it finished with us intrigued. We'd never gone so deep into anything like this before. It was us who wanted to know and by asking the experts we found out The experts at first made us nervous now there our friends. They've helped us and we hope we've given them our friendship and trust. I hope they feel the play is as much theres as ours

Guessing games in the Reminiscence Centre. Children think about life in the past.

4 UNDERLYING PRINCIPLES

Getting acquainted.

THE "NEED TO KNOW" PRINCIPLE: CONSULTING THE EXPERTS

Reminiscence work across the generations is based on the recognition of the older person as the expert. The children are starting from a situation where they **NEED TO KNOW** and therefore where the older people can make a positive contribution. They bring their own personal experience of life into the classroom as an aid to the children's understanding.

IMPROVING THE SELF-IMAGE OF OLDER PEOPLE

Many older people start out from the premise that they have little to offer to school children. This is especially likely to be the case when their own associations with school may be linked to fear or failure. When they see how interested the children are in what they have to say, and when they see the work the children produce as a result of their input, they feel valued and more integrated into their local community. They can see that they are uniquely qualified and enjoy being part of things in this special way.

GREATER MUTUAL RESPECT

When the children see the older people as sources of information, help and ideas, and when the older people see the children as creative, lively and appreciative, the result is a greater mutual liking and respect.

ACTIVE LEARNING WITH AND BY OLDER PEOPLE

Inter-generational Reminiscence is often just seen as question-answer sessions, but where the older people are working side by side with the children on creative and practical projects, often over several weeks, they are also "learning through doing", as well as understanding a great deal more about the way children think and the way their education is being planned.

LEARNING ACROSS THE CURRICULUM

Though history and English are the most obvious areas of the curriculum to which older people's reminiscences can contribute, it will be clear from the examples which follow that geography, science, technology, art and music can readily be incorporated. The different world of the 1920s and 30s which the older people describe from first-hand experience can reveal enormous changes in economic and industrial structures, in technology, and culture, as well as in moral values and social behaviour.

OLDER VOLUNTEERS COMMENT:

Lilian Burnett:
You are giving them a little bit of your experience. You can tell them and explain it and they're really hanging on what you're saying, as long as you're telling the truth, that's the main thing. You must tell them the absolute truth.

Joyce Milan:
What more wonderful audience can you have than children when they're listening to you? You get their attention and they're listening and they're intrigued. It's a wonderful feeling.

Bill O'Sullivan:
We show them what they cannot get from books. Nobody can get it from a book, what we know.

Dorothy Barton:
They learn that all old people are not idiots. That once you get older you have a great deal of experience behind you and you are capable of passing that experience on and not just capable of sitting in an armchair doing nothing.

Eileen O'Sullivan:
I find it gives me a lot of confidence when I tell the children my experience. I feel really great. I couldn't do that with grown up people, but with children I come over well and I feel as though I've done something.

Identifying opportunities within the National Curriculum for cross-generational activity

No matter which age group or subject you are working with, opportunities exist for cross-generational work.

SUBJECTS

English

Maths

Science

History

Geography

Modern Foreign Language

Technology

Music

Art

PE

(R.E)

SKILLS

Communication

Personal/Social

Study

Problem-solving

Numeracy

Information Technology

CROSS-GENERATIONAL ACTIVITY

DIMENSIONS

Personal & Social Education

Special Needs

Equal Opportunities

THEMES

Citizenship

Economics

Health

Environment

Careers

5 A NATIONAL CURRICULUM GRID

ENGLISH
Everybody has had some special times!
Apart from utilising communication skills, accounts of personal experiences form the perfect basis for drama or a written-up project.

SPECIAL NEEDS/ PERSONAL & SOCIAL EDUCATION
Just one meeting with an elderly person helps to make 'old age' a real thing for children, not a remote idea based on stereotypes.

ONE VISIT

HISTORY
With oral history part of the curriculum, the memories of older people are resources increasingly sought and valued. A first-hand account of life in World War II literally brings history alive.

GEOGRAPHY
One account of an elderly person's travels or place of origin can both inform and add a multi-cultural

MATHS
"It was two bob for a lamb chop then." As part of living dialogue, such remarks produce great motivation for children to convert from pre- to post-decimal currency.
A natural way into problem solving too.

ECONOMIC & SOCIAL UNDERSTANDING
Greater perspective on the world of jobs and money can provide the perfect context for young people to compare their own sense of good and hard times.

Older people jogging each other's memories as they handle objects connected with looking smart when they were younger.

Acting with older people is fun! These older people are remembering the excitement of seeing cowboy films at the Saturday morning pictures.

6 PREPARING THE OLDER PEOPLE

N.B. A useful guide to running reminiscence sessions is *The Reminiscence Handbook* by Caroline Osborn, published by Age Exchange.

Adequate preparation of both older and younger people for working together is crucial to the success of these inter-generational projects, so the following guidelines are offered, based on what has worked well in the past.

WHERE TO LOCATE THE OLDER PEOPLE

It is worth approaching local day centres, sheltered housing units, over 60s clubs, or community organisations to find a small group of older people who would like to co-operate on a schools project. Ideally the staff of such places will be willing to help with an initial 'brain-storming' reminiscence session in order to generate enthusiasm for the project.

For inter-generational projects to succeed it is important to establish a co-operative spirit between teachers and care workers, and to agree on certain objectives, since extra demands are bound to be made on the time and energy of both. If the project is on a specific subject, such as their own school or village, or a local industry, it is worth advertising in the local newspaper for people who would like to be involved.

INVITING GRANDPARENTS OR OTHER OLDER RELATIVES

Whether or not there is a local agency to help teachers, it will also certainly be worth approaching parents of the class to see if any have elderly relatives or neighbours who might enjoy this sort of contact. If so, be prepared to run a starter reminiscence session for them in the school or community hall to explain the ideas behind the project and to get the memories rolling.

A STARTER SESSION

The best preparation for older people going into a classroom situation of any kind is to involve them beforehand in a separate reminiscence session in order to build confidence. So many older people fear that they will have nothing interesting to say, that it is necessary to remind them that they have a fund of stories and experiences which are worth repeating.

If the preparatory session can be run in a group setting, this point will be easier to get across, since the potential contributors will realise that listening to the stories of others in the group is interesting, and that they can tell similar stories. Hearing other people's stories will of course be helpful in triggering more long-forgotten memories.

It is important to relate the reminiscence subject of the session to the work the older people will be doing with children in school, and to explain why the inter-generational work is being undertaken. What is their role going to be? What will be expected of them by the children and by the teachers?

A Reminiscence group sharing photos and memories - one person's memory sparks off another in an informal atmosphere.

LANGUAGE LEVEL

It is sometimes a good idea to ask the older people to retell a memory they have just shared with others of their own age as though it was a story for children, using simple words and plenty of expression. Our experience at Age Exchange is that older people learn very fast how to adapt their stories to the language level of the children, especially when they have been used to telling fictional stories to their grandchildren.

CONCEPTS OF TIME PAST

Concepts of time past will be particularly difficult to get across to small children. Their sense of the difference between the recent past and the past of their grandparents' childhood and the past of Anglo-Saxon Britain and the past of dinosaurs may be very hazy indeed. Grasping the idea that the older people were once young like them might need some thinking about, and maybe reinforcing with photographs, school books, etc.

It is a good idea to remind older people that many things which they take for granted will certainly be news to the children they are going to meet. This can be done by going back over some of the things which have been discussed and considering what will need explanation. For example, if the subject under discussion was home and family life when they were children, it might be necessary to explain to the children that fitted baths were not commonly found in people's homes in the United Kingdom, that toilets were often outdoors, that water had to be heated and that many tasks were manually done which the children might assume have always been done by machines.

It might also be necessary to point out that the mothers of many of the children they will be meeting have paid work outside the home, whereas the business of running a large family in the inter-war period and wide-spread discrimination would usually prevent married women from taking such work, even where it was available, and how attitudes to working mothers have changed since they were young themselves.

EVIDENCE

Encouraging older people to think what children would make of some of the bits of

The business of running a large family before the advent of machines was a full-time job.

memorabilia which they have held on to, will make the older person feel better equipped for the meeting. The objects and images will help them to engage the children's interest and involvement. For example a birth certificate, a picture of the older person as a baby and as a small child, a long-loved doll or toy will all help the children to grasp the difficult idea that they are talking to someone who was once as young as they are, and can share memories of that time with them.

If more than one older person is talking to the children, and their experience differs or even conflicts, they need to be reassured that this is useful for the class to think about. A variety of viewpoints will make the subject more interesting for the children. First-hand experiences are likely to be accurately remembered, but will reflect many different realities. The children can also analyse the information they are hearing and draw distinctions between what they might receive as fact and what they should question as opinion.

RESPONDING TO CLOSED QUESTIONS

It is worth warning the older people that children will often ask questions which seem to require only a one word answer, for example, *"Were your teachers strict?"* Of course a yes or no answer would do, but it is better to encourage the older people to see this sort of question as an invitation to recall particularly horrible or specially kind or really peculiar teachers. The children's questions can be used as a springboard. This will also make the child who has asked a question feel that her/his intervention was fully acknowledged.

A DIFFERENT CLASSROOM ATMOSPHERE

It is important to explain to the older people how very different the atmosphere is likely to be in the classrooms they will visit. Most of them will have a good idea about this anyway from their own grandchildren or from watching television programmes about education, but this point needs reinforcing for several reasons. It might prevent them from being too shocked at the apparent casual nature of teacher-pupil interaction compared with what they themselves experienced. It might also remove some of their fears that they are going to be expected to give a lecture if it is explained to them that they will be better understood by the children if they encourage the children to ask questions about the things which interest

A 1990s pupil struggles with sums in 'old money'.

them most. They should also feel free to ask their own questions of the children, for example, *"I have been telling you about the games we used to play, but what do you do in your play times?"* or *"I am remembering when I was very little. Do you have memories of when you were still too young to come to school? What is your earliest memory?"*

NEW APPROACHES TO THE CURRICULUM

The older people should be given some notion about the nature of the children's curriculum, so that they can see how their contribution is a valuable part of an overall strategy. This might seem a rather difficult thing to achieve, especially as many of us are still struggling to get to grips with the National Curriculum concept ourselves, but it would be helpful for the older people to know, for example, the underlying demands for knowledge, skills and understanding, and that they will be contributing in all three areas.

They will also need to know that although there are separate programmes of study for each subject, many teachers will be teaching several subjects simultaneously through the inter-generational projects. For example, an older person talking about starting work in the 1920s might well be assisting in teaching history, English, technology, maths, science, geography, careers education and education for citizenship without being aware of it all the time, and without separating out these elements at the point when they are reminiscing.

A POSITIVE EXPERIENCE

It is important to present the enterprise as an opportunity to make contact with children who want to meet older people and who need to know the stories they have to tell. They are going in as experts to situations where they can be of help, and so they can expect to be well treated by the young people they are going to see. Should this turn out not to be the case, it is important to make it clear to the older people that they are there on a purely voluntary basis and can withdraw if they are unhappy or uncomfortable in the situation without any shame or embarrassment.

Old style Arithmetic

Double Punishment - Painful Memories of Schooldays Past

There were times when I was top of the class for a few months, and then I'd be bottom of the class. The reason might be a different teacher I didn't like, so I didn't concentrate, or it might have been a time when I was larking about, which I'm afraid I often did, and had the cane for it. I used to screw up bits of paper and flick them across the room with the ruler, with messages written on them.

Once I was sent out of the room to another teacher. The whole lesson in that room stopped whilst that teacher said, "Yes, what do you want?" He probably knew anyway. You said, "Oh Mr. Ward I've been sent to you to get the cane". And all his class would prick up their ears, and you'd have to say what you'd had the cane for, " I flicked paper across the room instead of listening to history." "Ah yes. all right, fetch the cane for me then", and you had to stand in front of the whole of his class, so you had a feeling of humiliation, because there might have been some of your friends, there might even be your brother in that class, who's sure to tell your mother when you get home, that you've had the cane, so you get another one as well.

Milly Gardner

N.B. These extracts are taken from *Good Morning Children*, a book of schooldays recollections and photographs published by Age Exchange.

Date.	Name of Child.	Age.	Offence.	Amount of Punishment.	Signature of Teacher who inflicted the Punishment.	Head Teacher.
23-1-'24	Hook, Betty.	8	Laziness - Bad Work & Continual Lateness	One stripe on each hand	A. Rhoden	A.R.
29-1-'24	Hook, Betty	8	Laziness & Lateness	One stripe each hand	A. Rhoden	A.R.
30-1-'24	Hook, Betty	8	Laziness & Lateness	One stripe on hand	A. Rhoden	A.R.
11-4-24	Hook, Betty	8.	Destroying a book	Two stripes on R. Hand	A. Rhoden	A.R.
					G. Balmer Chairman of Managers Nov. 2186	
28-1-25	Butters, Joan	10	Continual Careless Work	One stripe on each hand	A. Rhoden Gellespott Chairman of Meeting March 8. 19 25.	A.R.
14-7-25	Butters, Joan	10	Very bad work.	One stripe on each hand	A. Rhoden	A.R.
16-9-25	Hook, Betty	10	Very bad work - laziness & rudeness	Two stripes on each hand	A. Rhoden	A.R.
1-10-25	Hook, Betty	10	Continued rudeness & laziness	Two stripes on each hand	A. Rhoden EHGoddardJones Chairman of Managers 25th Oct 1925	A.R.

7 PREPARING THE CHILDREN

THE LAWS OF HOSPITALITY

It is important to encourage the children to see the older people coming to the classroom as their guests, and to consider how they should be treated. For example, they should be offered somewhere comfortable to sit (which may mean bringing a different chair into the classroom) and a cup of tea on arrival.

Bearing in mind that the older people will think of a schoolroom in a very different way, it might be a good idea to ask a few of the children to begin by showing them round the classroom, explaining some of the work on display. Other children could be given responsibility for explaining what their current project is about and why they have invited the older person to the classroom.

AN AGENDA

It is certainly desirable to prepare in advance some of the areas for questioning which can be explored with the older people. This does not necessarily mean preparing the children with a fixed questionnaire, which might constrain them and prevent them from listening with an open mind to the stories of the older people. Their questions should flow naturally from what they have heard, but there does need to be an agreed framework. This can be arrived at by a brain-storming session with the children beforehand about what interests them and fits in with their classroom work, and what aspects of their own experience they wish to compare and contrast with that of their older interviewees. Once the main subjects for questioning have been agreed with the class, different groups of children can take responsibility for particular areas and work out more detailed questions together. This period of formulating questions can be a useful exercise in co-operative working and developing speaking and listening skills.

OPEN AND CLOSED QUESTIONS

The children should be encouraged to ask open questions which will elicit interesting answers from older people. This takes practice which can be in the form of a game, in which pairs of children ask each other questions which cannot be answered with a *yes*, a *no* or any other single word. Questions which include the words *who*,

---

Sticks and Carrots - Memories of Schooldays Past

I remember the teacher, when we were young, used to bring sweets in once a month . Thinking about it now, it must have been pay day. Anybody who'd been very good got so many sweets. Then you'd get perhaps a black mark and you'd get a sweet less, and that was an incentive I suppose. And these sweets were a luxury then as well because we didn't get all the pocket money that kiddies get now.

And as you got older the punishment we got was the strap. It wasn't the cane in Scotland. It was the strap, for girls as well as boys. I think your pride got hurt more than anything. And the worst thing of all was if you should cry in front of the class. You musn't cry. It was a sense of shame then if you cried. It was more than your life was worth.

And the boys used to pull their hands in sometimes and blow on them. They would hold their hands out for the strap, and they'd pull them in quickly and the teacher would get the strap on her leg.

We had a signature book and if you were extremely good you got a signature. And at the end of term there was a prize for the most signatures.

Edie McHardy

why, what, where and *when* are least likely to produce a *yes/no* answer, and phrases like *'can you tell us some more about that....'* will give signals to the older people that the floor is theirs and the children are interested. If the children find it difficult to formulate open questions, there is no need to worry, since most older people who co-operate in schemes like this will be ready to meet the children half way and will almost always offer full answers which respond to the underlying drift of the question, whether open or closed. It is a good idea to encourage the children to practise asking questions loudly and clearly and one at a time.

LISTENING AND REMEMBERING SKILLS

You might ask the children to practise interviewing each other and listening carefully to the answers, so they can say the information back afterwards. Listening carefully and remembering what has been said is just as important as asking the right questions. This is an area which tends to be taken for granted, but we know from our work with adults that listening is the most difficult skill to improve and is essential in reminiscence work of all kinds, regardless of age.

BODY LANGUAGE

If the children show clearly that they are listening, the older person is more likely to feel that they are being interesting, and therefore feel confident to say more, than if the children are looking around or whispering. They can explore the truth of this in pairs, with one person trying to continue talking, while the other looks bored. The speaker will almost certainly dry up very quickly!

RECORDING THE EVENT

Even small children can handle simple TAPE RECORDERS and they can then listen over again and discuss together the stories they have heard from the older people. There is of course, scope here for transcribing small sections of tape so that the original words of the speaker can be used in follow-up work by the children.

Where tape recorders are to be used, it is vital to have everything set up beforehand, and to have tested the machines, the batteries and the supply of tape. A better result will be achieved with a separate microphone which sits on a non-resonating base or fits into the interviewee's buttonhole some way from the machine itself. The tape recorder should always be tested before the

A classroom of long ago as remembered by an older person talking to children today. The clothes tell us a lot and so does the way the children are sitting.

recording session begins, and the date and names of those involved should be logged at the start. The tape should be clearly labelled immediately after the recording.

VIDEO is best suited to recording activity sessions and trips, or practical sessions where a skill or craft is being transmitted by the older people, rather than for 'talk' sessions. Some small video cameras are now so simple to operate that if children have access to them beforehand, they have a good chance of producing a satisfactory record of the reminiscence event. It is also essential to explain the purpose of the recording to the older people and to obtain their consent before proceeding. It is also a good idea to photograph the visit or other event, so that photographs can be interspersed with displays of work resulting from the meetings.

FOLLOW-UP

Even if older people visit the classroom just once, they greatly appreciate an invitation back to the school to see the work their visit has generated. If this is not possible for practical or organisational reasons, it is desirable that a small group of children take some of the work to the older people to let them see how they have helped. Letters of appreciation from the children are usually treasured by older people who have taken part in inter-generational projects.

A child views a visit to the Reminiscence Centre as a trip in a time machine.

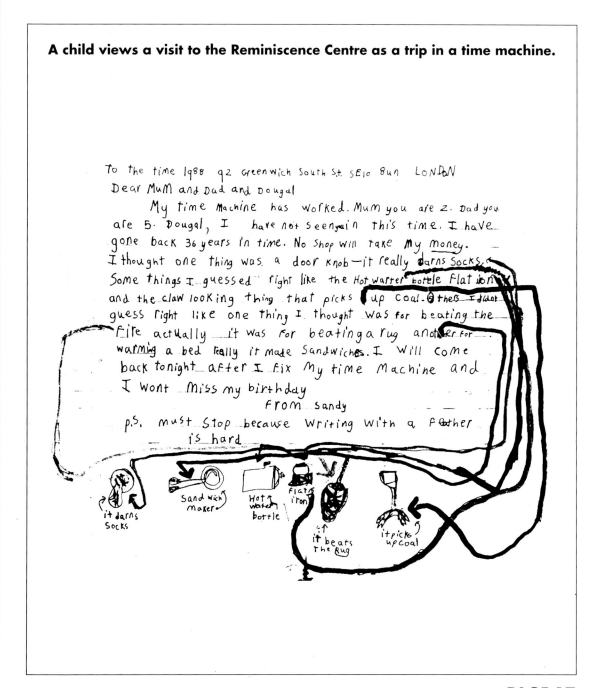

8 EXAMPLES OF DIFFERENT APPROACHES TO LEARNING THROUGH REMINISCENCE

LEARNING THROUGH GROUPS' WRITTEN REMINISCENCES AND PHOTOGRAPHS

Most of the projects described below involve a series of meetings between children and older people in the classroom or in the housing unit or day centre. However, where this is not possible, cross-generational work can take place through the written recollections and photographs of older people.

There have been an enormous number of oral history and reminiscence books published over the last ten years, many focusing on a particular locality, and others exploring a particular theme in social history or a particular period in the recent past. (A list of some of the most useful will be found at the end of the book.)

Through these written reminiscences, usually compilations of several people's stories, and the wealth of photographs which often accompany them, children can develop their understanding of a period, issue or area. Even though they may be working at one remove from the older people, the children will still get some sense of their life experience, especially since in many cases these reminiscence compilations are verbatim transcripts of interviews. This means they are often very colloquial in style, may even be in a local dialect and certainly retain some of the immediacy of spoken interchange when read aloud in class.

We are astonished at Age Exchange how far-reaching is the use by schools of our compilations of reminiscences around themes in social history, such as health, education, evacuation, unemployment, starting work, etc. The first-hand stories of the pensioners are often juxtaposed in the classroom with official reports and history book versions to help school children with the interpretative aspects of history in the National Curriculum.

The stories are also used as a preliminary to actual meetings with older people to focus the children's minds on key subject areas. The photographs are used to examine clothing and environments and different social relationships, and to make comparisons with present day equivalents.

'Clara's Story '- a troubled tale of growing up in a 1930s orphanage, by Age Exchange Youth Theatre - based on an older person's autobiography.

Clara's dream by Age Exchange Youth Theatre children. Imaginative work based on an autobiography of an older person.

WORKING FROM ONE PERSON'S AUTOBIOGRAPHY

One particular example of a project which grew out of a written source was a play called "Clara's Story", created by children aged ten to fourteen in a Youth Theatre group run by Age Exchange.

The children had expressed an interest in making a play about an orphanage. It so happened that Age Exchange had been sent an autobiography (one of many unsolicited manuscripts which we receive each year) of a woman who grew up in children's homes and foster homes around London in the 1920s and 30s.

Extracts from this story were photocopied for the children, read aloud and discussed. They based their improvisations around these passages. The director also represented the writer, answering the children's questions from her knowledge of the story, since it was not possible to reproduce the whole book for all the children.

Eventually the children put the play on for relatives and friends, using scenery they had made based on photographs supplied with the manuscript and ideas of their own. The writer of the original reminiscence piece and her husband and family travelled three hundred miles to see the show the children had made from her memories. She was hugely delighted and moved by their efforts and felt that she had been thoroughly heard through her writings. The children had a tremendous sense of commitment to the material, knowing how difficult the woman's early years must have been, and that she was coming to London specially to see their work.

The writer sent the following letter:

Dear Pam,

Thank you all for a wonderful evening. I think the children performed very well and enjoyed themselves at the same time. What a wonderful bunch of kiddies! I wish I lived nearer to be able to take advantage of any future performance. Thank you again for giving my writing a little recognition.

Yours sincerely,

Clara Chesterman.

COME AND WATCH HISTORY ON TELEVISION WITH US!

A very modest example of introducing older people into a primary classroom has been tried when a junior school class were watching the popular Yorkshire Television series *"How We Used To Live"*. Two local pensioners who enjoyed the programmes themselves and who belonged to a reminiscence group which met near to the school, agreed to visit the class every week and watch the programmes with the children. They gave comments and feedback from their own life experience and thus demonstrated the reality of the footage. In effect they were saying, *"This is not a story; it is real and we lived through something similar when we were younger"*.

In the course of these weekly meetings, a relationship was established between the children and the older people, and they often stayed on in the classroom to help with resulting written work and drawings, sometimes bringing in photographs of themselves at different stages of their lives, or press-cuttings of particular local events which related to the television programmes.

This activity certainly meets the requirements of Key Stage 1 History in that it helped the children to understand the concept of time passing and the world changing. Through talking and listening to older people who had different views of the same experience, they built up the idea of history as a variety of lived experience forming a complex picture.

The photographs and press-cuttings were evidence which helped to give the past a reality for the children, and prevented it from seeming like a story. And by seeing pictures of the pensioners as children, the class had to struggle with concepts of ageing and change.

One can readily imagine using a similar strategy of inviting older people to follow a television series (perhaps *"The People's War"* or one of the other great documentaries on World War II which might be used in a Key Stage 3 History project) with a class of secondary pupils, and the opportunities this would create for interviewing and for assembling evidence.

When I was little we had stone hot water bottles to heat the bed.

Lil Murrell talks to children about her own childhood.

Schoolboys make life tough for the sweetshop man on the way home from class. The children's drawings and acting are all based on older people's stories.

COME TO OUR CLASSROOM AND TELL US ABOUT OUR SCHOOL IN YOUR DAY!

Another very small-scale initiative which gave rise to a great deal of work in a junior classroom was the invitation to two people in a nearby sheltered housing unit to visit the school and talk about their own memories of learning in that school.

The children prepared many questions before the pensioners arrived, and the pensioners themselves had been involved in a reminiscence discussion with others in the sheltered housing unit about their own schooldays. These memories had been prompted in a reminiscence session by a small collection of objects, including a slate, a dip-in pen, an old school exercise book with copper-plate writing, a school report and a ruler.

The older people began by showing the children round the classroom as they remembered it. They described the physical arrangement of the furniture, including the teacher's high desk, and the maps and diagrams which were on the walls. They described the school day with all its rituals (nose-blowing, deep breathing, drill, etc) and what the atmosphere was like in the classroom. The children were particularly interested in punishments and descriptions of vicious teachers.

Conversation strayed into childhood games and out-of-school activities, with the children fascinated to hear what sweets the older people liked and how they all had to walk to school and back twice a day as there were no school dinners. This raised the question of how their mothers had to be at home to provide a meal at lunchtime, and how relatively few mothers had paid work outside the home compared with today.

The children experimented by moving the furniture around to see what it was like to learn in a different arrangement, and they played some of the playground and street games which the older people had told them about. They wrote about their new understanding of childhood in the past and drew pictures of the older people they had met as youngsters and of the teachers they had heard about. They did some sums in old money and handled the actual coins.

The visitors were invited back into the classroom to see an exhibition of the children's work and to listen to an assembly by the class based on the work they had done together. Being guests of honour at a school assembly was a good experience, and one they were proud of. The children's work was then displayed in the sheltered housing unit's communal lounge.

Of course the same project could have been followed with older people who had not attended that school, but who had gone to an elementary school in the area. However, for children and older people there is a certain extra excitement in visiting the actual classroom where they spent time so long ago. The memories are more likely to be jogged by the surroundings than if the same exercise is conducted on territory which has no associations.

Where it is possible to consult the school log book for the period covered by the older people, and to look at their own school reports and exercise books (which a

surprising number of people have kept), there is a heightened consciousness on the part of the children as to the nature of their own style of education and the many changes that have taken place for better or worse.

Some years after this project, Age Exchange created a reminiscence book called "*Good Morning Children*" about schooling in the 1920s and 30s, and many schools have subsequently used the book in connection with work on their own school's anniversary. Where schools are reaching a fifty year landmark or even a centenary, it is obvious that listening to the school memories of older local people will enrich the sense of community and of continuity. It will also contribute to Key Stage 2 of the History Curriculum (learning about changes in everyday life by asking questions, organising information and presenting the results visually and in writing.)

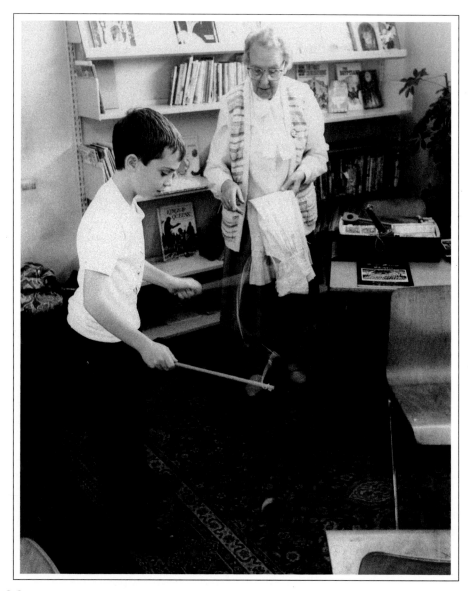

Lilian Burnett demonstrates the diabolo in Lee C of E Primary School, South East London.

THIS IS YOUR LIFE! LIFE STORY WORK IN SCHOOLS

Another way of linking an older person and a group of children is by working on the story of one person's life through her reminiscences. A country school in Somerton in Somerset worked with one older woman from a nearby residential home, and made a book about her life in pictures, poems and stories.

The teacher used this work to encourage the children to explore the concept of change in their local area, by comparing their interviewee's life in the village with their own. The older person concerned was a member of a small reminiscence group run by one of the care staff in her home as part of a year-long Reminiscence Project run by Age Exchange, but this special contact between her and the children gave her the greatest satisfaction, and the children's book of work became one of her most treasured possessions.

Mrs. Barber remembered:
At harvest we always had lovely food brought to the field to eat. The men would drink a lot of cider. I would drive the horse to the Royal Oak and carry out two gallon stone jars of cider. Well, one day I went and it was just too much for me. I slipped as I put the jars down in the cart and down came the cider and jars all over me. I had to go home and tell my mum.

one year She drove to the Royal oak

When Mrs Barber Pulled away one toppelled off and smashed

A pupil from Chard in Somerset imagines country children in the past.

Working with a slate and slate pencil from a Reminscence Box on Schooldays.

Eileen O'Sullivan talks to children about washday in the past.

9 WORKING WITH OBJECTS

Local museums often have handling boxes which are available to schools, or the Age Exchange Boxes can be hired very cheaply for short periods. Alternatively teachers can assemble their own boxes of memorabilia and artifacts around a theme, but this can be a time-consuming and even costly business, now that there is such a commercial market for ephemera of all kinds.

Lil Murrell & Lilian Burnett unpack a Reminiscence Box with pupils at Lee Church of England Primary School in South East London.

WHAT'S IN THE BOX?

Another form of classroom visit by pensioners is the handling session, which has become very popular with schools in the vicinity of Age Exchange. Two volunteers visit a classroom with a box of thematically grouped reminiscence items. The theme is determined by the teacher to fit in with on-going work in the classroom from a range of Reminiscence Boxes available from Age Exchange. Older people who have been involved in this project comment:

Lil Murrell:
I don't think I could stand up and teach children a whole class at a time, but I don't find it daunting to stand up in front of a class with a Reminiscence Box. I think it's because I'm talking from experience and there's a difference between doing that and actually doing a teacher's job.

Joyce Milan:
The boxes are a real success, because the children are handling the objects and taking in what we're saying. And it helps us for the

continuity because if suddenly you dry up and think what can we talk about next, you can pick up something else and think oh right, I know what I can tell them about this.....I took the Schooldays Reminiscence Box to a group of eight year olds in a special school where they were mostly in wheelchairs and quite seriously affected. I let them put the old satchel on and put things in it from the box and they were thrilled to bits.

WAYS OF USING A REMINISCENCE BOX

There are many ways of using these handling boxes in the classroom. The following have all been successfully tried, depending on the focus the teacher requires:

■ the children examine the unknow objects and try to deduce their function.

■ the children put them into different groups, according to use, weight, material, area of life.

■ try to imagine what the modern day equivalent object might be if such a thing exists, and if not to try to work out what change or discovery has made the object redundant.

■ children choose an object which interests them and say everything they can about it, such as what they think it is made of, its weight, texture, smell, where it might have come from, what it might have been used for, what sort of person might have used it and in what connection, and what meaning the object has for them.

■ the children tell a story in which every object in the box is featured. They have to work in groups of four to eight and the story has to make sense.

■ a small group pretend that the box is theirs and explain who they are and why everything is there.

■ the children undo the box in a group role, for example as:

i) a group of archaeologists from the year 2,200 trying to learn something about early twentieth century life,

ii) a group of detectives who are trying to trace a missing person, and this box, found in a left luggage office, is all that remains of them, so what can they learn about the person from the box?

■ the children select an object by feel from a pillowcase or bag. They describe what they think it is like, its size, shape, texture, imagine its smell or taste and colour, and only then pull it out and identify it positively. As a language development exercise this is a very stretching approach.

■ the children look at the object and then they are covered over, as in the Pelmanism exercise/game. See how many the children can remember. This will involve considerably extending the children's powers of descriptive language. If this exercise is attempted both at the beginning and the end of a session, it will be clear how many more objects are remembered by the children once they have been discussed and given linked meanings and names.

OLDER PEOPLE AS GUIDES

Older people visiting the classroom with a Reminiscence Box can demonstrate the use of all the objects and encourage the children to ask further questions about who would use these things, when and how. They might then tell the children what memories are associated with it for them. For example, a Reminiscence Box entitled *"In The Kitchen"* might contain amongst other things

■ *a pastry cutter*
■ *a candle*
■ *coal*
■ *a mousetrap*
■ *a fly paper*

and each of these objects will have an association for the older person. This will enable the children to draw a mental picture (or an actual picture) of what a kitchen would have been like in the days when their

visitors were children of their age, and when a mother's tasks were radically different from those of their own mothers.

Dorothy Barton, an older volunteer comments:
What I find fascinating is the sort of wonderment on the children's faces when you're talking. I was talking once in a room to small children about the lack of fridges and freezers and things like that to keep our food in, and how we had a fly paper hanging up. I explained to them about the fly paper and they thought that was absolutely disgusting. It was disgusting I suppose, but it was the only way we had of getting rid of flies.

A *Childhood Games Reminiscence Box* will give the children a great deal of food for thought as to how older generations of youngsters passed their time with no television and almost no money. As older people describe the streets where they played (and the very little traffic to disturb them), the cramped houses which hardly contained their large families, the neighbours who kept an eye on their play and who were sometimes the victims of games like "Knocking down Ginger", children will begin to form an idea of a very different social fabric from the one they know themselves. This is of course in line with components of Key Stages 1 and 2 of the National Curriculum for history, as well as taking in elements of design technology, science, English and art.

It is important to include some games and toys which come from other countries and cultures and descriptions of how they were used, and some home-made toys which can be easily copied. In this way, a *Childhood Games Box* can spark off comparative cross-cultural reminiscence, as well as demonstrating that some objects are common across cultures. Playing with the contents of such a box can also give the children ideas for games they can make and play themselves using available materials, as well as giving rise to discussion about how the materials in use today in the U.K. might be different from those traditionally used.

One exercise which is fun to do with children around a *Childhood Games Box*, is to ask them to prepare a box of objects to show the older people, which would represent the games and activities which are important to them. Each child brings in an object (or if it is too difficult to carry or too precious to bring in, then a drawing of the object will do) and explains the significance of the object to the others in the class and to the older people. A variant on this is to involve the children themselves in some reminiscence about their favourite toys and the games they played when they were very

small. A lot of good discussion can arise about changes in lifestyle from comparing the contents of the older people's box and that created by the children.

John White, a Year 6 class teacher comments:
The children gained a great deal from the Age Exchange experience. This is one of the few mechanisms available that make the past real for children, enabling them to empathise and gain a much deeper insight into the past.

Laura Brittan, a pupil, comments:
When Age Exchange came it was fun. They told us things they used to do when they were at school. It was very interesting. Now I know how different schools are now than then..... The ladies were very kind and nice.

Michaela Sutherland, another pupil, adds:
The ladies said they was always on time, and when they were naughty they got a slap on their hand with a ruler. We played marbles and we played with a spindle. Soon they left and we clapped and said Bye.

Other Reminiscence Boxes which Age Exchange have put together include *At the Seaside, Looking Good, The Home Front in World War II, Family Health, School Days,* and many more. (See appendix for full list.)

Pupils and the narrator, Lilian Burnett, pose a picture based on her story. This is a good way of starting an improvised scene based on memories . Make 3 pictures and then join them together with action and diologue.

These Boxes which contain between twenty and thirty small objects and notes as to what they are and how to use them, were originally developed for use by nurses and care staff who work with older people in hospitals and homes to trigger reminiscences and to encourage social contact between residents. We have been surprised how schools have taken up the Boxes for their own use, and now have our own schools project whereby older volunteers will visit schools to share their memories with the children using the box contents as a focus for their discussions.

Margaret Phair, an Age Exchange volunteer, writes:
Last week I went to the school to talk to the children about the war. I had a ration book, a gas mask and an identity card. It was amazing what they didn't know. They didn't know what a searchlight was, or how all the railings were taken down during the war. Their teacher said that this was a class you couldn't talk to, but their faces lighted up with interest. I get a great deal of satisfaction from this. It gives me a real inner glow.

An older Caribbean woman has kept this photograph of her grandmother.

She has passed on all her grandmother's stories and recipes to her own grandchildren in London.

A translator of the future listens in South East London to older people's memories of growing up in India.

STORIES FROM OTHER LANDS: OBJECTS REFLECTING DIFFERENT CULTURES

Reminiscence Boxes can reflect different cultural backgrounds as well as different historical times. A collection of objects which emanate from the Caribbean or from India will raise even more questions in the minds of an enquiring class. What are these objects and what do they tell us about the culture, society and geography of the place they come from?

So many questions will be difficult to answer that it will be desirable to invite older people to come to the classroom and explain the contents of the box to the children. Again, the older people will be the experts, and where they do not speak English, the children in the class who do speak their language may emerge as skilled interpreters.

An imaginative assortment of objects and images will open the door for discussion of many different aspects of daily life and culture in another part of the world, as well as things which are unexpectedly similar. This will create many more questions in the minds of children concerning things they might have taken for granted before, and think are the same all over the world. An example here might be the discovery that not all schooling takes place indoors in special buildings, and that not everyone learns to write with pens on paper. Hearing the explanations and the associated stories and personal memories of the older people will open up many curriculum areas, including spoken and written English, geography, science, religious education, history and music.

Age Exchange Reminiscence Box - *Born in the Caribbean.*

A SPECIAL REMINISCENCE OBJECTS CORNER IN THE CLASSROOM

Following a performance by the Age Exchange Theatre of a play based on older Indian people's memories, children in a South London primary school went on to work with a group of older Asian people who met near their school. They devoted a special corner of the classroom to memories, objects, fabrics, photographs, religious items, herbs and spices, musical instruments, documents and drawings relating to the stories told by the older people. In this way, an Indian village corner was made including models of the houses laid out in relation to natural features. This led on to celebration of certain Indian holy days and the preparation and eating of appropriate foods in the classroom.

One can readily see how the involvement of older people in a project of this kind will contribute to many of the cross-curricular themes (Environmental Education) and dimensions (Personal and Social Education, Multi-cultural Education) in the National Curriculum guidelines.

Of course it would be possible to pursue a project of this kind with no input from an older person or group of older people, but there can surely be no doubt that the project will be more meaningful and satisfying if the journey of discovery for the children is through people as well as objects, and that those people are their guides and friends on a fascinating journey.

It will be enormously valuable for the children to understand, through the life stories of one or two older people whom they get to know over a six or seven week period, how and why many other people moved from Indian villages, for example, to English cities crossing thousands of miles and very great cultural and language barriers in the process.

Sharing this knowledge with others in the school by presenting the work in a special school assembly increases the status of the project and of all the people involved. It is something to celebrate, and the older people are the guests of honour.

The work can then be taken and shown to the rest of the ethnic elders group, so that they too can see the possibilities which are open to them by sharing some of their stories with local children. Where the resulting presentation involves some kind of dramatisation or music and dancing, it is likely to be even more warmly welcomed by the group of older people, and might well open the door to further joint activity.

Parkfield JMI School
St. Davids place
Hendon London
NW4 3UB
1st March 1993

Dear Age Exchange Theatre,
    The song that you sang to the baby was familiar because my dad used to sing that to me. My friends and I enjoyed your performance. We really enjoyed your dancing. We liked the sounds you were making at the beginning we liked the bit when

Kutar came to England and when he was working. We liked the instruments and when we told our parents about the play they wish that they came watch it
    Your sincerly

Beejal Hina
and
Joshna

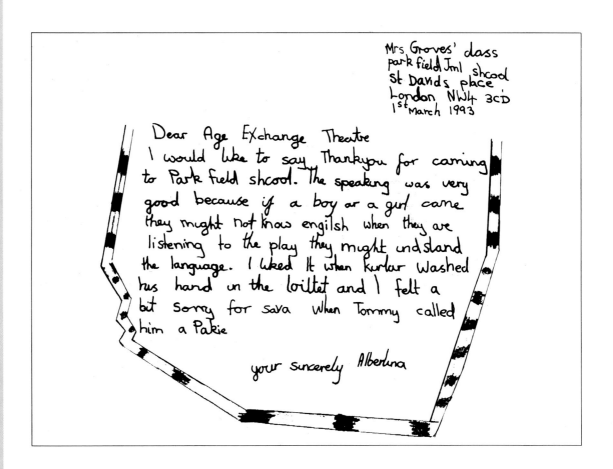

Mrs Groves' class
park field Jnl shcool
St Davids place
London NW4 3CD
1st March 1993

Dear Age Exchange Theatre
I would like to say Thankyou for coming to Park field shcool. The speaking was very good because if a boy or a girl came they might not know engilsh when they are listening to the play they might undsland the language. I liked It when kurlar Washed his hand in the loillet and I felt a bit sorry for sava when Tommy called him a Pakie

your sincerely Alberlina

Routes by Age Exchange Theatre was based on memories of older Punjabi people living in London. It played widely to multi-ethnic groups of children in London schools.

Photographs from *On The River* by Age Exchange. There is no traffic in the street, so the children can play there. The River Thames is a thriving place of work with huge ships docking daily and thousands employed in now vanished trades.

Photos courtesy of the Museum in Dockliands Project

10 THE TOPIC APPROACH TO INTER-GENERATIONAL WORK

A PROJECT ON TRANSPORT WITH 7 YEAR OLDS

An East London primary school had chosen transport as their topic, and were keen to invite older people to the classroom to meet the requirements of history Key Stage 1 and to encourage communication skills among their older infant groups. Age Exchange arranged two reminiscence training sessions for staff, who then tried the following approaches in the classroom:

Older people visited children in the classroom. They remembered different kinds of transport which the children may never have heard about such as trams, steam trains, river steamers, barges, ferries, horse-drawn vehicles, tandems, open cars and open-topped buses and produced photographs to show the children what these looked like.

They recalled the sounds and smells of the streets in the days when they were children and there were far fewer cars on the road and probably greater safety. Some of the sounds they remembered were the clatter of trams, the snap of ticket punches, horns, hissing steam trains, fog horns from the ships on the river, and of course all the street cries which might have been heard by people selling their wares on foot or horse-drawn vehicles. Smells recalled were tar on the road (with its associated healing qualities for chest infections) jam and other foodstuffs in preparation in local factories, roasting chestnuts, horse dung and many others which brought the atmosphere of the time alive for the children.

They compared their journey to and from school with those taken by today's children, who in turn described the sights, sounds and smells they particularly notice in their area.

The older people talked about the work of their fathers, brothers and husbands in various trades relating to transport such as the railways, the docks, blacksmiths and farriers, bus and tram drivers, lightermen, barge builders. They discussed the position of women in relation to this sort of paid work (ie. most mothers working in the home, with larger families to look after, fewer domestic appliances, the need to provide a main meal in the day time, the husband's income often uncertain or inconsistent.)

They talked about the speed of life when the older people were young. How long did it take to get from A to B? How far afield did they travel in their young days? Did they go on holidays or was it more often a day trip by steam train or river boat or on a bicycle? The older people took a joint visit with the children to the Railway Museum at North Woolwich.

They discussed the changes in transport they had witnessed: the coming of air ships and aeroplanes, changes of transport during the war years, and their first trips to a foreign country.

Active learning by primary children at the North Woolwich Railway Museum in London with Age Exchange performers and older people.

A PROJECT ON MY HOME TOWN WITH 9-10 YEAR OLDS

Maerdy is a small town in the Rhondda Valley in Wales which used to be centred on the coal mining industry, but where the pits have recently closed. There is a strongly felt need to preserve and protect the history of the town and to maintain a sense of pride among its residents of all ages. Some older people of the town had already contributed their memories to a book about the local mine, but a group of fourteen older women were enthusiastic about recording their own reminiscences in weekly sessions with the help of the local community arts team. Age Exchange was invited to develop an intensive three-day project, involving these women, the community arts team and a group of fourteen children from a local primary school with their teacher. The project would culminate in a joint performance and party, in which a sense of the past could be conveyed in a creative spirit.

The older people talked with the children about their childhood days in the town, and they began work on a large backcloth (4 feet by 24 feet) representing pre-war Maerdy. The children also produced creative writing focusing on questions like, *What would life have been like for me in Maerdy in 1930?* and *How have things changed, especially for women?*

In a group, the older people shared memories around the following themes:

Place: the house you lived in as a child, and a place you would like to go back to

Time: a time when you were happy, and a difficult time in your life

People: a person you loved, a childhood hero, a person in the past whom you disliked

Values: the beliefs you live by and your message to the children of today.

From the stories which emerged, a series of life history portraits were made, in which a photo of the older person was surrounded by their memories. The children used these life history portraits as the basis for improvised dramatic scenes.

By the third afternoon, after three very full working days, the backcloth was completed and hung along one side of the hall, the life story portraits were arranged as an exhibition, and the children's work was on display. The final presentation was as follows:

Children's games, past and present, performed in mixed groups

Scenes from family life (elders playing parents and grand-parents, and children playing the older people when young)

Dancing old and new, ballroom, country and disco-dancing

Songs (traditional songs and hymns and Welsh songs)

What came out of the project was an increased sense of the identity of the community, a great deal of enjoyment for both groups, a lot of learning for the children in the fields of history, English, art, fashion, environmental education and industrial understanding.

> **Older people, reminiscence workers, a community project and a class of children - all worked together on the Maerdy project - an Age Exchange programme in the Rhondda Valley, Wales.**

A PROJECT ON WHALING WITH 11 YEAR OLDS

Another topic approach to reminiscence work in the classroom was tried with Year 7 pupils in a South East London secondary school. The boys were reading poems and stories about the sea in their English lessons (including "The Rhyme of the Ancient Mariner", "Flannan Isle" and extracts from "Moby Dick".) They became very excited by the topic of whales and whaling.

A local man who had worked as a whaler agreed to come to the classroom and talk to the children. A.L. Lloyd was an excellent story-teller, filling the boys with awe and wonder at the different world he was describing. He was also a well-known singer of folk songs. He taught the children whaling songs with story verses and rousing choruses. From the songs he sang, which, often reflected a much earlier period than he could in fact remember at first hand, the children learned a great deal about work and everyday life aboard a whaling ship in different periods, and also about the attitudes and emotions of the men who were involved. Some of the boys' poems reflect the words of the songs they learned, and reveal a high level of identification with the material, bringing their own ideas.

Further, the class made the mental link between folk songs or work songs which had passed down through an oral tradition and the stories about his own past life in the 1930s on a whaling vessel which Mr. Lloyd was now passing on to them. He talked about working life aboard a whaling ship, pay, pecking orders, conditions and attitudes. He gave a lot of fascinating detailed information about how the whale was caught by the highly paid gunners on the catcher boats, how it was flensed and broken down on the huge factory ship and

what the various parts and by-products were eventually used for.

This led the children on to look at the whales in the Natural History Museum, and to find out about the efforts of the International Whaling Commission to control catches. Some of them acted out a trial of a captain of a pirate whaling vessel using information supplied by Mr. Lloyd about the dependence on whaling of certain geographical areas, and from the Save the Whale campaign literature on endangered species, and the need to protect the whale from extinction. The project involved the class in many areas of learning: environmental geography, science, technological changes, spoken and written English, music, oral history, and even religious education in the sense that the boys were tussling with moral dilemmas and identifying with a variety of viewpoints (eg. the ordinary sailor, the harpooner, the captain, the girls ashore, the international conservation committee on whaling and, of course, the whale itself).

Eventually the boys performed for the rest of the school a multimedia piece about whaling (including some electronically produced whale music they made in a sound studio after hearing recordings of whale song, and a giant cardboard whale made in art lessons to go with the project) and A.L.Lloyd came along to lead the singing.

Song: The Bonny Ship the "Diamond" - taught to the boys by A.L. Lloyd

The "Diamond" is a ship, my lads, for the Davis Strait she's bound
And the quay it is all garnished with bonny lasses round.
Captain Thomson gives the order to sail the ocean wide
Where the sun it never sets, my lads, nor darkness dims the sky.

Chorus:
And it's cheer up, my lads, let your hearts never fail
For the bonny ship, the "Diamond" goes a-fishing for the whale.

Along the quays of Peterhead, the lasses stand around,
Their shawls all pulled about them and the salt tears running down
Now don't you weep, my bonny lass, though you be left behind
For the rose will bloom on Greenland's ice before we change our mind.

Chorus:
And it's cheer up, my lads, let your hearts never fail
For the bonny ship, the "Diamond" goes a-fishing for the whale.

Oh, it'll be bright both day and night when the whaling lads come home
In a ship that's full of oil, my lads, and money to our name.
We'll make the cradles for to rock, and the blankets for to tear,
And every lass in Peterhead sing: Hushabye my dear.

Chorus:
And it's cheer up, my lads, let your hearts never fail
For the bonny ship, the "Diamond" goes a-fishing for the whale.

Poems by three 11 year old boys

i) The night I left I felt so sad
That I had to leave my love
To go off to Greenland
And hunt the big monster
I must go and hunt the big monster
Because I am desperate for money
As I lay on the deck
Listening to the sound of the flute and the accordion
I see a whale
I am a harpooner
I leapt to the bow
I threw the harpoon
It stuck right in his back
It was a catch
When I got back the captain was glad
He gave me some rum
Then I went back to port and my girl married me

ii) I looked back at the harbour
I remembered what I had done
I wish I'd never done it
I kept on telling myself it was not my fault
She made me do it
She kept on nagging me
She deserved to be left
Suddenly I was told to scrub the decks
I put my knees down on the deck
It was so hard
My legs were in blisters
My hands red, so raw
That night, I laid in my bunk
I rocked from side to side
My hands so sore
My legs so sore I am so tired
Oh why did I come?
But in the back of my head
I knew I had to stay
I knew I had to

iii) A hump-backed whale and her baby
Were swimming in the cool deep blue sea
When she heard a splash
It was a whaling boat, plain to see
The mother and her baby swam for their lives
But the boat got nearer and nearer
And the splashing got louder and louder
The baby was swimming to survive
The mother protecting her baby
Let the harpoon pierce her side
And in the now dark red water
She steamed at the boat in revenge
While the mother died protecting her baby
The whaler was damaged and sailed blind
And the baby swam away
Knowing the world was not always kind.

A RIVER WORK PROJECT WITH 15 YEAR OLDS

A project built around older people's memories of their working lives can be a fruitful approach to aspects of geography and technology in the National Curriculum, as well as making a valuable contribution to understanding the history of the local area. It is also a very useful means of addressing the Environmental Education and the Economic and Industrial Understanding components of the cross-curricular themes. A recent reminiscence theatre project, *On The River*, by Age Exchange about the River Thames as a working river in the 1920s and 30s led to some good meetings between retired river workers and school pupils. Performances in schools were attended by retired lightermen and dockers who told the pupils about what the river looked like in its heyday, how materials were handled and lifted, how the river was navigated, how foodstuffs were stored and shipped and what health hazards were encountered.

The obvious changes in technology emerge when a lighterman compares rowing a barge up the Thames or tugging a ship into port with transporting the same cargo by lorry along motorways, but there are also important environmental issues raised by these discussions, which prevent pupils taking a simplistic view that progress has been linear and that only gains result from industrial change.

Charles Wegner and Andy Andrews in *On The River*, a touring theatre show by Age Exchange based on memories of the Thames as a working river.

Building site teaboys - a first job remembered from the 1930s.

A PROJECT ON STARTING WORK WITH 16 YEAR OLDS

Other reminiscence projects with schools around the theme of *My First Job*, have supported the Careers Education and Guidance cross-curricular theme, as the pupils heard about work practices in the past, apprenticeships, health hazards and union issues as these applied in their own area fifty or more years ago.

Extract from an older person's memory in my *My First Job* by Age Exchange

I was a van boy for Lovibonds and we used to serve all round Silvertown, all round that way. Lovibonds - the brewers. I'd start at 8 o'clock in the morning, and perhaps I wouldn't get home till 2 o'clock the next morning. I got 10 shillings for that. Many a time I walked from Barking to the Blackwall Tunnel, with a light showing the carman the kerb, with it being so foggy. Sometimes in them days, you couldn't see your hand in front of your face. And then when you got to the Tunnel it was nearly as bad in there. With the old wagons going through there; used to be a proper pea-souper. Sometimes the Woolwich Ferry never used to run if it was foggy. You had to go all round Tower Bridge. Horses then; it was all horse-driven. Some nights it had been so bad we had to keep out all night... You just went home and had your wash, then you'd come back and start again. If you weren't there, there was somebody else to take your job. Ten bob a week. Course we used to get a few tips now and again.

The above example of a memory of starting work as a delivery boy prompted pupils to discuss with the older man why he put up with these conditions, what he did with his earnings, what other jobs were available to him and how long he stayed with the firm. It also raised environmental questions about pollution in London, about the adverse effects of certain kinds of fuel, about speed of travel, other kinds of danger, health hazards and insurance which pupils had not thought about.

Work available to girls leaving school at fourteen in the past was obviously much more limited than today, and there is much scope here for older and younger people to compare prevailing attitudes and personal expectations in relation to women's working lives. Stories about older people giving their earnings directly to their parents and receiving a small amount back for their own use are often shocking to young people and lead to interesting discussions on family relationships in an economic context. The stories of the many women who started their working lives in domestic service provide much discussion material on changes in social structures and increased social mobility.

The change in the kind of work available to women once the war started has proved another excellent topic to explore with older people in the classroom. Women remember the opportunities presenting themselves from 1939 onwards and how they responded to new openings. They have also discussed with pupils the withdrawal of those job opportunities at the end of the war, and how they reacted to returning to the domestic situation.

A HOME ECONOMICS PROJECT FOR 16 YEAR OLDS

Older people who have not had paid employment outside the home can also contribute to pupils' Economic and Industrial Understanding and Health Education. For example, a group of girls studying Home Economics for GCSE examination invited an older woman to the classroom to talk about her understanding of home economy.

Mrs. Wilson was a woman who had brought up eleven children on an extremely tight budget which was wont to fluctuate as her husband's work came and went. She visited for an afternoon and talked at length about how she ran her kitchen, how she budgeted, what she did to spin out limited rations, where she shopped, what ingredients were available, how she preserved food, etc.

The pupils were most impressed with Mrs.Wilson's grasp of home economics and hygiene, and realised that she had many domestic skills which they knew nothing about. They stayed for half an hour beyond their school day to listen to her (a tremendous compliment had she but known it!) and the visit resulted in some unusual course work. This included the pupils trying out some of her recipes with mixed results!

Other school groups have also attempted **JOINT COOKING SESSIONS** with older people in day centres and homes, often trying out forgotten country recipes and writing them down before they disappear.

A group of older people in a Somerset residential home enjoyed remembering the meals of their younger days, and made a small recipe book which the local young people found fascinating. The assistant head of the 30-bedded home, Janet Rowe, writes:

We welcomed the opportunity of the Age Exchange project to generate stimulating conversation into an otherwise routine-filled day. Some of the recipes have been adjusted for modern cooking purposes after we had experimented with them in our kitchens and had several disasters. Accurate weights and measures were not available in many households, and often the residents described 'a bit of this' or 'a handful of that' without being able to specify the quantity. And oven temperatures then were governed by the heat of the fire at the time of baking. We hope you will find these recipes entertaining to read, fun to try and a challenge to eat!

Older people reminisce about the countryside i wartime.

Remembering country life - pensioners tell children about picking hops for beer in their younger days.

RECIPES USED DURING THE PROJECT

Breakfast Brawn

Ingredients

4 pigs feet
2 ears
2 sheeps tongues
½lb. fresh pork

1 small onion
1 blade of mace
cold water
pepper and salt
2 cloves

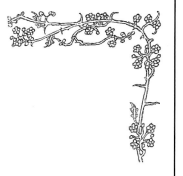

Cover all the meat with salt and leave for four or five days then add enough cold water to cover. Add salt and pepper, onion, mace and cloves. Bring to the boil and simmer for three hours. Take out the tongues and skin them. Chop up all the meat while still warm. Put into a flat-bottomed mould with cold water and a little of the liquid. Place a plate on the top to weigh it down and leave for 12 hours before cutting.

Elsie's Pudding

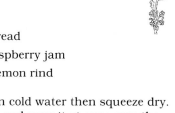

Ingredients

1 pint milk
2 eggs
½lb. stale bread
½ teacup raspberry jam
1 teaspoon lemon rind

Soak bread in cold water then squeeze dry. Boil the milk and pour it at once over the bread. Add the jam and beaten eggs. Pour into a buttered basin and steam for 2 hours.

Poor Man's Goose

Ingredients

1 slice of fat bacon
1lb of pork trimmings
2 large onions
1lb of potatoes cooked and mashed
½ teaspoon chopped sage

a little gravy
salt and pepper

Chop and fry all the meat. Chop and fry the onions separately. Line a pie dish with the mashed potatoes, put a layer of meat, then a layer of mashed potatoes. Bake for one hour. Serve with apple sauce.

A wartime family scene played by pupils from Swanmead School, Ilminster in Somerset.

11 THE PARTICULAR MERITS OF WORKING THROUGH DRAMA

Making a play is actually one of the best ways of working between the generations, because the children are going to need all the detailed information they can get hold of from the older people, and they are going to have to translate it into another medium. They have to take the material and look for a way of conveying it through their drama to others who were not present at the initial telling. They cannot just regurgitate what they have heard, and they cannot work with generalised impressions; they must appropriate it sufficiently to make a new creation from it.

The **NEED TO KNOW** principle is reinforced further when part of the intended audience for a children's drama presentation is the older people themselves. The play must pass muster with them, and again this puts the older people in the position of helpful experts. In every example of this method, the older people become very involved as sources and directors, as audience and constructive critics.

A STUDY OF WORLD WAR II THROUGH PLAY MAKING

A study of the local community is a key component of the history National Curriculum, but when this study is undertaken through inter-generational work it complements the history syllabus at every stage, whether it be through adults talking about the past in Key Stage 1 or Britain since the 1930s in Key Stage 2, or wartime Britain in Key Stage 3. It also obviously complements the speaking and listening elements of the English curriculum, as well as more general underlying communication skills and social relationships.

A project in Somerset developed by Age Exchange involved 11-13 year-old children in a middle school in the making of a play based on the memories of older people in their village during the war years. The older people attended a lunch club at the school, and they agreed to help the children to make a play.

The older people told their memories and wrote down additional stories for the children. They dug into their photo albums and their old boxes of memorabilia. The resulting classroom work cut across many areas of the curriculum, but all were bound together by the great enterprise of the play.

The teacher, Wallace Parfitt, writes: *We used local history from first hand evidence to inspire English work and a play. Meetings with the older people were scheduled in lesson time. I suggested scenes around which the children could improvise. These scenes were based on stories which had emerged from conversations with the pensioners and also on my knowledge of the children's own needs and experiences. The visitors became the experts, watching what the children did, suggesting story developments for the scenes and improved dialogue, as well as offering helpful ideas on songs, costumes and scenery. In effect, they became the producers of our play, filling in*

A Somerset pupil is fascinated by old photos brought into school by the 'experts', and produces her own version.

with their comments the children's understanding of that period. In the final production, one of the pensioners was the narrator.

We achieved cohesive relationships and mutual understanding between diverse age groups. Everybody enjoyed this contact, and as well as direct learning, the children have developed a more positive view of the elderly and gained from the positive view the elderly have of them.

The effect of this project on a small community was quite striking, in that friendships grew and doors were opened for all sorts of other communications between the school and older members of the community. The play was also featured at a special Age Exchange Reminiscence Festival, entitled "When We Were Young", in South Somerset, where it was seen by groups from many other villages as well, and the children obviously derived enormous satisfaction from the work.

Pupils from Swanmead School, Ilminster in Somerset, recreating the Second World War from older people's memories.

<u>What I got out of age exchange</u>

A few months ago our class started talking and working with the elderly people of Ilminster. The elderly ladies told us all about there life during the Second wond war. When we got to know to know the elderly ladies we started to put together a long and realistic play about the Second world war. The play starts in a farmhouse Kitchen in Ilton, where a family of four were sitting down to there evening meal. The play carrys on and alot more happens. The play is along play so everyone is involved in some way. The work on the play began in our classroom but the ladies couldn't manage the steps so we started to use the Couminty lounge. When finially the play had all been acted out this was after along time of practising and been told what was right and what was wrong we had together a really good play on the second war. What I thought was really good was that the elderly bales would share with us there remanisacines, however sad and lonley it made them feel. Overall I think during this time I have gained a better and clearer understanding of the second world war

Rebecca Woodburn

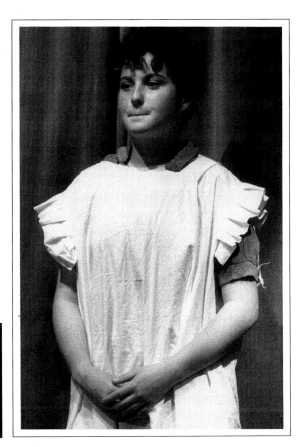

Solo G.C.S.E. Drama project. Telling the story of one older person's life.

A GCSE SOLO DRAMA PROJECT FROM SOMERSET

A growing number of schools have developed their own projects for senior students which have depended on inter-generational reminiscence work. One example was an individual study in which a Somerset pupil spent many hours with an old lady in a home and created a one-woman show from her life story in which she played the part of the older person and all the characters who were important to her.

This remarkable achievement was presented at the same reminiscence festival mentioned previously and gave many of those present ideas for developing similar projects themselves.

Children from Chard in Somerset in a play with older people based on memories of their young days.

TWO ADVANCED LEVEL THEATRE ARTS PROJECTS FROM LONDON AND THE ISLE OF WIGHT

WHEN YOU WERE OUR AGE

In a South East London girls school, six pupils studying A Level Theatre Studies decided to make a play about what it was like to be seventeen years old before the war. They visited six older people in a local sheltered housing unit over an eight week period and interviewed them about their lives when they were young.

There was much interchange between the two groups of information and stories and a good working relationship was established. The girls tape-recorded and transcribed all the interview material and made their play out of the stories they had heard. They rehearsed with the older people, and eventually put the play on for all the residents of the sheltered housing unit. The girls' social and communications skills were considerably enhanced by the whole process and the older people enjoyed their involvement in the project and the resulting entertainment. They were pleased that their efforts had helped the girls to an A grade in their exams.

ISLAND MEMORIES

A similar experiment took place on the Isle of Wight which has a very large population of older people. A mixed sixth form set from Ryde High School undertook to work with older people through a local community arts agency (Independent Arts, who had trained in reminiscence work with Age Exchange) to make a play about the island and the town of Ryde in particular through local people's memories.

The pupils did their research in old people's homes in the locality, going out in small groups to investigate particular topics such as school days, shopping, work on the island, the war years. The arts agency arranged for willing older volunteers to meet them, to show photographs and to have their memories taped. The pupils transcribed the tapes and began to prepare scenes around the different themes.

Age Exchange trained the pupils in ways of

converting these memories into theatre, including the notion of using the actual words from the interviews as the script for some scenes, or as words for a song to go with another. They spent the rest of their drama lessons that term preparing with their drama teacher a first rate piece of reminiscence theatre. They toured this to the old people's homes and played it to the school to everyone's satisfaction. In the process, there is no doubt that their own and other people's consciousness was raised of the older people as a valuable part of the community. Their excellent exam grades were a reflection of their whole-hearted commitment during the project.

Fitting this sort of project into an A level timetable does require special commitment from pupils and their teachers if the older people's involvement is to be more than token. Making the visits at times convenient for older people is not always easy given the demands of the school timetable, but in all cases the effort has been considered worthwhile and the results particularly rewarding for old and young alike.

Ryde High School students in their play, *A Pocket Full of Dreams.*

TWO YOUTH THEATRE PROJECTS UNDERTAKEN OUTSIDE SCHOOL TIME

In 1986, Age Exchange set up a specialist Youth Theatre where local children could meet every Saturday morning to make plays based on older people's memories. Since then, there have been two productions per year, and always older people's stories have been the chief source materials for the plays. The National Association of Youth Theatres has recently become very interested to promote this area of work as part of building more caring communities and enriching the sources on which young people draw for their inspiration.

There are many different ways of working with the older people on these plays, and I shall give two contrasting examples which might be of use to readers. All the projects undertaken by the Youth Theatre could work equally well in a school environment.

THE BLITZ SHOW:

In this instance the children and the older people worked in parallel. The children worked from the older people's stories as described above, and the older people prepared their own scenes about living through the Blitz. At first the older people improvised their lines and then a script was produced from these improvisations. They attempted to learn the script, but found this extremely difficult, so they reverted to improvisation, and were full of admiration for the young people's ability to remember. At the performances, the two groups alternated their scenes, and there were readings interspersed from the older people's book of stories about the Blitz. This was an award-winning project, and although it was quite difficult organisationally, it was an exciting new direction for young and old alike.

Living Through The Blitz

A collage designed by children from photos and memories. It was used as the front cover of a book of older people's memories and as the basis for a painted backdrop.

AGE EXCHANGES

IN SERVICE:

For this play, two older people who had been in domestic service wrote down their stories for children in the Youth Theatre, and these were used as a basis for improvisation, together with written stories from the various Age Exchange Reminiscence books (see appendix for full list). The children improvised around these stories and then invited the older people to attend a session and add to what they had done. This led to additional material being added in and greater accuracy being achieved.

The two stories were very different, since one woman had loved her years in service and been very well treated, and the other had hated every minute of it and felt thoroughly humiliated by it. This contrast was useful for the children to hear, and their play reflected a range of experience, including other stories from the children's own relatives. The play was costumed and suitable props were borrowed from the Reminiscence Centre and the children performed to eighty relatives and friends one weekend with the two older people as honoured guests.

Two pensioner volunteers comment:

Margaret Kippin:
It can be quite painful, because you've suddenly told the children something about a part of your life that you weren't very happy about and they enact it, and when we came to see the In Service play you know, there was a little lump there because it brought it back. It wasn't all laughter all the time when we were young, although when you look back on it you think of the happy times more than you remember the sad times. Actually, some of those kids were the same age as I would have been, they were fourteen, weren't they? They were extremely good. The fact that they've taken in what you've told them and they have interpreted it their way, they alter it a bit for various reasons but they really put it over extremely well. They're very good. The shows have been lovely.

Of course the older people have to accept that the children will interpret their stories very broadly and they cannot afford to be too precious about the way characters are represented by the children.

Margaret Phair:
Don't you think that each child, as an individual, when they're asked to do a character, that they put their own personality into it. So if they're going to act the part of a Gran, they bring their own Gran into that character or one that they've seen on television, and put that together with what we've said.

In Service Youth Theatre show by children from Age Exchange.

12 THE REMINISCENCE THEATRE IN EDUCATION MODEL

This relatively new approach to inter-generational work involves considerable planning and resourcing, but teachers have found it to be one of the most positive approaches yet devised, giving rise to a tremendous amount of cross-curricular follow-up work in the classroom. It is a development of the strategies employed by professional Theatre in Education companies, and its particular emphasis is on creating a rich environment for story-telling and drama work between children and older people.

A theme is chosen which will engage the children in local schools, and which will involve them in meeting older people who have many memories to share. Three such themes have been explored so far: *school days in the 1920s, the evacuation of London children in 1939, and hop-picking by London families before the war.* All these themes have a strong childhood experience element with which today's children can readily empathise. A professional team of actors, director and designer interview many older people and record their memories. These memories become the basis for the play, a designed environment and an accompanying book of edited memories and photographs. The designer creates a three-dimensional environment at the Reminiscence Centre which will stimulate many memories for adult visitors, and will give young people an immediate sense of the period and the place.

GOOD MORNING CHILDREN

For our first TIE show in the Centre, the gallery was filled with old-fashioned double desks with inkwells, a high teacher's desk, dip in pens and blotting paper, slates and slate pencils, maps, teaching aids and diagrams from the past and a thunderous wall clock. The children (30 each day from different primary schools) spent the morning learning, 1930s style, under the fierce scrutiny of the charismatic Miss Hood, played by a professional actress. All the activities the children performed (such as breathing exercises, drill, times tables, copper-plate writing, geography exercises and mental arithmetic) were suggested by the pensioners at the Centre, and based on the exercise books, photos and memories they had retained from their own schooldays.

Just as significant as this recreation was the sub-plot which emerged by adding another actress to play a child, a device which enabled us to raise certain social/historical issues with the children.

Good Morning , Children

Learning 1930s-style in the Reminiscence Centre.

The girl in the third desk with the plaits is a 'plant', an actress in role.

Elsie, the brightest pupil in the class, has just won a scholarship to the high school, and Miss Hood speaks proudly about printing her name in gold letters on the school board of honour. But when Elsie turns up late, having had to help her hard pressed mother with the younger brothers and sisters, she is not excited about the news and it gradually emerges that she is not going to be able to accept the place. Money for books and uniform would still have to be found, and her family cannot afford it, with no regular income. The father also believes it will be more important to save what educational opportunities there are in the family for Elsie's brother who he thinks will make better use of them. Elsie is torn between her family's view and Miss Hood's outrage, and the children are left alone with her (in her role throughout) to tussle with the arguments. Again, this story was a common one relayed to us by older people now working in the Centre as volunteers. At the end of the morning, the situation remains unresolved, but a great deal of discussion has occurred between the actors and the children on

Miss Hood puts the children of 1991 through their paces 1930s - style at the Age Exchange Reminiscence Centre.

Ink monitor for the day at the Reminiscence Centre *Good Morning Children* project.

equal opportunities, on family relationships, on unemployment and how it affects families and on ambitions and dreams.

In the afternoon, the children met the older people on whose stories the play was based, and in small groups prepared scenes based on the stories they told about their own schooldays. Follow-up work arising from the day covered history (the changing position of Britain from Empire days) English (much speaking and listening and maintaining a position in a discussion, as well as writing tasks) maths (sums in old money and handling old coins) music (songs taught in schoolrooms in the 1930s) and cross-curricular themes: Economic and Industrial Understanding, Education for Citizenship, Careers Education.

Lil Murrell, a volunteer comments:
I think the schools project was one of the best, because the children were actually taking part. We were teaching them what it was like to be in school in our days, and they were reliving our school days. I think it registers more. If, when we were at school, we'd actually acted out scenes, instead of just learning the dates of history and the wars and all that, I think if we had actually acted out the scenes of those things that happened like the children actually living our school days, actually doing it and taking part, I think it would have stayed in our minds a lot longer. It's a lovely way of learning. It's very effective. And wasn't it good fun for us to work with the children on that project!

HOPPING MAD

For our Theatre in Education project on hop-picking, the gallery had real hop plants running from floor to ceiling in front of a mural of a hop-field painted along two walls, giving the effect of a three-dimensional hopfield. There was plenty of hop-picking paraphernalia borrowed from a local museum and from ex-hop pickers, photographs, printed memories and we made a little pub at one end, so that everyone remembered what the hops were actually picked for and where some of the hoppers' earnings were spent! Two corrugated iron sheds were erected outside to represent a hop-picker's hut and a cook-house with a real fire and cooking pot in it. The huts were furnished entirely by the older people who had contributed their memories for the project, so when they eventually showed the children round in role, it really did feel like their own hut.

The actors and director developed a scenario which lasted over a school day, and which involved a single class of children in a dramatic recreation, and a group of older people who took on roles for a short part of the day and acted as story-tellers. Each day a different school visited the project, getting involved in a series of adventures created for them by the actors, such as trying to raise the money for the fare to get to the hop fields, negotiating for the hopping hut they wanted, debating the rate per bushel with the farmer's representative, and considering the serious consequences of strike action.

They learned a lot about the living conditions of poorer Londoners in the '20s and '30s, especially in the dockland areas of London, and the historical and economic context in which a stay at the hopfields of Kent could constitute the highlight of a child's year, and an essential opportunity for their mothers to earn a bit of money to buy winter clothes for the family. They also learned that older people can be fun to work with in drama, and can maintain their parts in an improvisation really well because they know what feels right to say in the situation from first hand experience.

Professional actors, old people and children spend a day in a specially prepared environment, exploring memories of hop picking through theatre, drama and story telling.

Hop-picking

When we go hopping
we work till were dropping
And there we go Shopping For tea

It Made Me feel Sicker
To look at that picker
Because he was quicker than me

by Robert + Wayne

The follow-up work again cut across many sections of the National Curriculum. Most obvious was English (spoken English through all the discussion in role, upholding an argument and listening to stories, and written English in the many poems, letters and other pieces of creative writing to emerge as a result of the children's strong identification with the material) but a great deal of art and maths resulted, and areas of technology were covered as the children learned about the disappearance of hand-picking in the face of mechanical advance. This latter piece of knowledge was learnt quite differently as the children now understood what the loss of hopping as a way of life would have meant to Londoners who looked forward to it so much each year.

A pensioner volunteer wrote:

Kathleen Ash:
I think it showed them a completely different way of life that we had in those days: that you earned your money, that nothing came easy, that you had to really rough it. All these conditions that you lived under when you went hop-picking, cooking out in the open, living in a small hut, nothing there at all, no proper lavatories, sleeping on straw, I think it showed them a completely different way of life. I think they enjoyed the excitement of taking part in it. You can generate the excitement yourself by telling them what it was like, and they feel they're living through it with you.

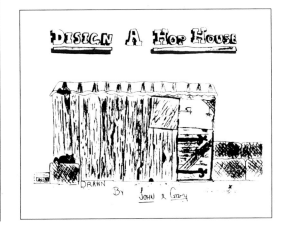

DESIGN A Hop House

DRAWN BY John & Gary

Bill and Eileen O'Sullivan in the recreated hopping hut they helped us to furnish for our hop-picking project. They enjoyed sharing their stories with groups of school children.

GOODNIGHT CHILDREN EVERYWHERE

Perhaps the most powerful stimulus so far came from our *GOODNIGHT CHILDREN EVERYWHERE* project on evacuation of children at the start of World War II. The 8 to 13 year olds who took part in this project were certainly covering important aspects of National Curriculum history syllabus (Key Stage 2, Britain since 1930 and Key Stage 3, the era of the second world war) but their follow-up work showed they had covered important parts of the English and geography syllabus and had produced creative writing and art which revealed real identification with the experience of the evacuees they met and worked with in such a rich physical and emotional environment.

Some pensioners involved in the project comment:

Dorothy Barton:
If the children act out the story themselves, I think it gives them a good idea as to what the child, say it was an evacuee, what the child must have felt at the time, being taken away from home. It gives them more of an insight into what that child's mind had felt than if they just read it.

Margaret Phair:
They've actually got tears, oh they were upset.

Joyce Milan:
They were choked...Especially when they split brother and sister up....."Don't take me away from my brother!"

Lil Murrell
They actually lived those parts, those children, especially the ones who were left behind in the billeting centre, the ones no-one picked. They really felt that. Those children felt what it was like.

Evacuees leaving London for the countryside at start of World War II.

A haunting image from Age Exchange book of memories, *Goodnight Children Everywhere*.

It may strike the reader that these Theatre in Education days initiated by Age Exchange are highly ambitious projects which would be difficult to reproduce in schools, but in fact we know that schools have used the ideas and produced home-grown versions of these programmes. An example was a school where the class teacher took the children through the evacuation experience, using our scenario as a guide, and asked local older people to help on the re-enactment. And several schools have followed our schooldays programme in their own classrooms, with teachers undertaking some of the role play themselves. There is no copyright on good ideas, and the intention in publishing these exercises is that teachers and community workers should use whatever suits their situation from the suggestions offered.

Children taking part in the evacuation project relive the experience of boarding a train to an unknown destination.

A 1939 evacuee drawn by Lisa from Rushey Green School, London in 1990

A CHILD AT WAR

13 INTER-GENERATIONAL VISITS TO THE REMINISCENCE CENTRE

The Reminiscence Theatre in Education events are run for limited periods only, but we operate an on-going programme of school visits to the Reminiscence Centre. Schools say what themes they are pursuing, and we arrange for children to meet in the Centre with older people who are happy to talk with them about that theme from their own experience, helped by the abundance of resources, objects and images at the Reminiscence Centre.

Again, the intention in outlining this area of work is that where schools are not able to visit the Centre but have a nearby collection or museum of twentieth century life, they may find our inter-generational experience helpful.

Eileen Taylor, the Reminiscence Centre worker responsible for school visits, writes:

Initially the Reminiscence Centre worker discusses the visit with the class teacher to ensure that all relevant areas of the topic will be covered during the one and a half hour session. Sometimes a teacher will want to do a topic connected with the 1930s and 1940s, but will not be sure which aspect would be most beneficial. Then the Centre worker can advise, bearing in mind the age

of the children and type of project work already undertaken and completed. Then the centre worker contacts trained Age Exchange pensioner volunteers, and depending on the type of visit, recruits two to three pensioners. There are more discussions with these volunteers on the exact content of the visit. For example, if a teacher wants the "Shopping in the 1940s" visit set in World War II, then the emphasis will be on rationing, the non-availability of certain food stuffs, and the welfare foods service.

The Reminiscence Centre has the fixtures and fittings, and stock from an original shop, as well as a kitchen range, gramophone and shelves of memorabilia which can be used in a variety of different ways with schools. It is important to point out that although some visits may take place in the main area of the centre, this is not always the case. There are occasions when the centre worker starts with an empty room in another part of the building, and with some imagination and use of a Reminiscence Box, an Age Exchange exhibition or posters, old newspapers and photographs can transform the space into an interesting and stimulating setting.

Dorothy Barton talks about washday with children at the Reminiscence Centre.

A SAMPLE INTER-GENERATIONAL SESSION AT THE REMINISCENCE CENTRE

A session covering *The Old Shop* and *Paper Packaging* and *Storage* is one example which might prove useful to readers. N.B. We always try to include pensioner volunteers in the planning, as they usually have lots of ideas and suggestions, and often loan some of the items.

List of items needed

- Glass or plastic sweet jars quarter filled with old fashioned sweets.
- Weighing scales with weights
- Butter pats and butter or margarine
- Grease-proof paper
- Biscuit tin with glass lid, or tin with no lid
- Broken biscuits
- Red lentils, butter beans and pearl barley
- Loose tea (not tea bags)
- Loose sugar
- Bundles of wood (try hardware shops/petrol stations)
- 1 notebook and pencil for mother's shopping list
- 1 cup (1d worth of pickle, pickled onions, jam)
- 1 shopping basket
- 1 string bag
- paper bags in different sizes
- newspaper

Other items could be added i.e. pictures and photographs and postcards of old fashioned shops.

THE SESSION

The Old Shop

This could have an emphasis on the lack of refrigeration in the home and the need for mother to go shopping every day, which could lead to a discussion on how women's lives have changed.

Talk about the time it took to queue at each counter for service, and the types of shops mother would have to visit to get all the family's shopping.

For young children watching a pensioner demonstrate the butter pats and having a try at weighing and patting up the butter can be fun. Some other children could use the weighing scales for the sweets, tea, sugar and pulses. The cup was often given to a child with a penny (1d) to run to the corner shop at lunch time and tea time for a small amount of jam or pickle, which was often all that mothers could afford. Selling such small amounts made the shopkeeper more money than selling the whole jar. Broken biscuits were sold cheaply, and were considered a treat, especially if some were chocolate or fancy biscuits. Some of the old fashioned sweets are still sold today, so it should be relatively easy to find - gobstoppers, lemon sherbets, bulls eyes, whipped bon-bons, fizzy odd-balls.

Packaging

Packaging in the past is discussed with the children. They learn how to make a poke (conical bag for sweets, etc) and discuss how products were packaged by the shopkeepers before the omni-present advertising which we now take for granted. There are environmental, technological and health issues here as well as social questions about time and money available to shoppers and disappearing skills in the retail trades.

Uses of Newspaper in the home

Newspaper was used in the home in a variety of different ways. Children made paper spills to light father's pipe/cigarettes, or a candle/gaslight. Paper twists were made to lay the fires, and there are a variety of different twists for pensioners to demonstrate. Newspaper was cut in neat squares, a hole pierced through a dozen or so squares, then twine inserted and ends tied together, to be used in the outside toilet or privy. By encouraging the class to make these items, the children will gain an understanding of some of the many tasks their grandparents were expected to do each week. How may uses does newspaper actually have? The list is still being added to at Age Exchange.

An exercise that can be fun and informative is the "Brainstorming" session where children and pensioners discuss old and modern uses of newspaper and then call out while the teacher writes the list on the board. The children can then be encouraged to look at the long list and put it into headings, for example:

Uses of Newspaper Remembered:

- To read - for information/knowledge

- To clean - with vinegar to clean windows

- To insulate - under carpets/lino

- To decorate - paper cut-outs for shelves

- To contain/hold - paper bags or paper mache containers

- To preserve - with mothballs for furs/woollens, etc

The special feature of these sessions is that one is working alongside a pensioner who has actually experienced the areas covered

Children visit the Reminiscence Centre and handle objects.

by the topic, and can tell the children what life was really like for them. Those stories and answers to the many questions that the children will ask, make the topic come alive and sustain the interest of the class.

Wendy Hamilton, a class teacher from St Patrick's R.C. Primary School in Plumstead, writes:

Given the constraints of finance on schools, and the emphasis of specific subject-based targets for the National Curriculum, school visits have to be planned and budgeted for much more carefully nowadays. I took 33 year 4/5 children to the Reminiscence Centre.

I had discussed in advance the areas the children had covered, and I was given some choice in what was offered to them on their visit. After some discussion with Mrs. Taylor we opted for 'Paper and Packaging' and 'The Old Shop'. Earlier in the year the class had done a science topic on materials, which involved looking at the various properties of paper, wood, etc. We had also been involved in a can recycling project in connection with McDonalds.

The class topic for the half term our visit occurred was 'Britain since 1930'. The areas covered by Age Exchange were perfect for supplementing this topic area, and the children were able to relate their experiences and knowledge gained during their visit to work done in the classroom.

The pensioners who talked to and worked with the children presented the information very well, and the children related well to them. I feel that the opportunity to meet and talk with members of the older generation, who are not their relatives, is of equal importance to the knowledge acquired during the visit.'

Centre volunteers comment on the school visits:

Bill O'Sullivan:
The reason I come to the Centre is for the school children and the thing that I'm amazed at really is that the children really pay attention to what we're saying and what

we're doing, and they really love it here. I've had postcards and letters from the children from the schools to say how nice it is to come here. They can enjoy the things they've never seen in their lives before. Or they might say, 'My grandmother had one of those but I never knew what it was for until we were shown by you. I said to them one day that my mother had six children, three boys and three girls and we all used to sleep in one bed. The children went uurgh..., and one little girl said to me 'How did you sleep then?' I said 'Well we had the three girls with their heads at the top and the three boys with their heads at the bottom, and we used to sleep and sleep beautiful'. They don't realise, they can't read that in a book. They don't realise that these actually happened.

A child's record of a visit to the Reiminiscence Centre.

USING REMINISCENCE OBJECTS WITH CHILDREN WITH SPECIAL NEEDS:

Groups of children with physical disabilities often visit the Reminiscence Centre. One teacher reports on a visit by Charlton Park School pupils:

Ruth Boxall:
The class are 7-9 years old and all have physical disabilities. Some have no speech and use Bliss Symbolic Alternative Communication. The children enjoyed their session at the Centre. They are looking at families now and in the past. Joyce showed them the artifacts on the Reminiscence Centre worksheets and talked about how they were used. Also the toys she played with. They also talked about the range and tried out the change machine in the old shop. They had fun working the stairlift themselves.

Follow Up: That afternoon we played with toys I had previously bought from the Reminiscence Centre and talked about what Joyce had told us, whilst playing. The children took the worksheets home and told their parents (in speech or symbols) about the artifacts on the sheet. Several parents reported enjoying this homework.

The teacher and the children wrote to Joyce afterwards:

Dear Joyce

I enclose a letter we wrote as a class. The words are the children's and we worked together on the spelling. They really did enjoy their visit and learned a lot. We've been following up in school and they took their worksheets home and told their parents about the stone hot water bottle, the tongs, etc. Their parents wrote down what they said and enjoyed being part of things. We read "Peepo" today and commented on the coal shed, etc. Many thanks for the sensitive way you involved all the children.

Yours sincerely,

Ruth Boxall.

Joyce Milan working at the Reminscence Centre with children from Charlton Park School - sitting round the range.

Joyce Milan talks to children from Charlton Park School about stone hot water bottles.

The children's letter:

Dear Joyce

Thank you for showing the things at the Reminiscence Centre to us. Joe liked the small iron. Mark liked the shop with the lever (rapid wire system) and so did Jamie. Kyle liked the lift in the shop. Wayne liked the old record player. Sonia is sad she missed it. She went to the airport. We hope we see you again.

Love from

Mark, Kyle, Joe, Jamie, Wayne and Andrew (and Sonia).

Joyce Milan and Finlay Finlayson both enjoy the children's visits. They comment as follows:

Joyce Milan:
I've helped with several visits to the Centre by children with learning disorders and physically disabled children and I've found this most rewarding. They love to handle the things that you show them, They're sitting in wheelchairs mostly, but they can use those tongs that pick things up, and they do love you to explain how they're used. They have great difficulty in following what you're saying but gradually and gradually, you realise that they are following it. One or two do small drawings of the items and you can recognise what they're drawing as well.

Finlay Finlayson:
I've been taking the special needs children. What I get from this most of all is watching the children. To start with they're like any other kids, wondering what they can touch, they're not a little bit interested. Here's this old fogey sitting in the chair about to talk to them.......and gradually you see their faces light up and their interest change. As I say cheerio to the children, the amount of them who suddenly say to me, "I'm gonna fetch my Gran in here". And they do bring their grandparents back. Granny suddenly takes on a new image.

14 CONCLUSION : MAKING MEMORIES MATTER

In all the examples of inter-generational work outlined in this volume, the older people have been invited to participate because they can contribute to the children's understanding through their life experience. In other cultures wisdom is thought to reside with older people and they are the revered holders of their community's history. We have lost this concept, but inter-generational projects go some way towards restoring a sense of the importance of older people's role in society and the need to value them. The children gain a stronger sense of their own cultural identity, their own past and the way in which their present has been shaped by it. By making memories matter, we can work in the present through the past for a more enlightened future.

Lil Patrick, a pensioner from Bermondsey, South London, sums it all up:

We were brought up with extended families around us and that was the way that history was passed on to us , but that is not the case today. We are the last generation of that extended family community. Our children are 'down the line', as they say, which means that they've moved out of the area for one reason or another. And so it's important for us to make sure that our history is recorded. Our personal history. We're handing on living history. We're still living it and we're handing it on to the next generation, and hopefully they'll do the same when they get to our stage in the game.

It is a moment of excitement when an older person sees her memories in print for the first time.

15 APPENDICES

BIBLIOGRAPHY

Generation to Generation by Maureen O'Connor, pub. 1993 by Cassell.
ISBN 0 304 32588 0

Talking Time by Maggie Hewitt and Annie Harris, pub. Learning by Design,
Tower Hamlets Education, Professional Development Centre, English Street, London E3 4TA
ISBN 1 873928 89 0

Link Age Primary Schools Pack (forthcoming) from Link Age, St Margaret's House,
21 Old Ford Road, Bethnal Green, London E2 9PL

Oral History Journal, Issue on the National Curriculum (spring '92)
pub Oral History Society, c/o Sociology Department, University of Essex,
Wivenhoe Park, Colchester, Essex, CO4 3SQ

Introduction to Oral History In The National Curriculum by Allan Redfern,
published by Oral History Society, 1993.

Lifetimes by Caroline Osborn and Pam Schweitzer, pub. 1987 by Age Exchange, 11,
Blackheath Village, London SE3 9LA

The Reminiscence Handbook by Caroline Osborn, pub. 1993 by Age Exchange
ISBN 0 94786 19 3

AGE EXCHANGE BOOKS OF PHOTOS AND MEMORIES

Fifty Years Ago (memories of the 1930s)

What Did You Do in the War, Mum? (women's wartime work)

Can We Afford the Doctor? (health and social welfare before National Health Service)

Across the Irish Sea (memories of London Irish older people)

A Place to Stay (memories of pensioners from many lands)

Remedies and Recipes (Caribbean health and diet)

Good Morning Children (schooldays in the 1920s and 30s)

The Time of our Lives (leisure time in the 1920s and 30s)

Goodnight Children Everywhere (memories of evacuation in World War II)

When We Were Young (Somerset rural memories)

Our Lovely Hops (memories of hop-picking in Kent)

My First Job (memories of starting work in the 1920s and 30s)

All Our Christmases (Christmas memories 1920s-40s)

Just Like the Country (London's inter-war cottage estates)

A Day at the Fair (Blackheath Fair in 1920s-40s)

On the River (memories of working on London's river and docks)

Living Through the Blitz (Londoners' memories)

Grandmother's Footsteps (forthcoming book of reflections by older people and children on their grandparents)

Prices on request from Books Department, Age Exchange, 11 Blackheath Village,

London SE3 9LA Tel 081 318 9105

AGE EXCHANGE REMINISCENCE BOXES

Teachers from all areas of Britain have spotted the potential of the Age Exchange Reminiscence Boxes as unique educational resources. Many of the boxes provide excellent source materials for project work on core study units of National Curriculum history, geography, science, technology and English.

Since starting the Age Exchange Box Scheme which was developed for use by older people, we have been surprised by the interest of so many teachers. We have therefore developed special notes for teachers using the boxes, offering guidance as to the contents of the boxes and how to use them in the classroom. Also, we have developed the Victoriana box specifically for schools.

Reminiscence Boxes Now Available For Hire

with some examples of their contents

1. Childhood Games

Street, playground and rainy day games and rhymes. Older people will enjoy this box. Their younger friends will be fascinated.
Skipping rope, diabolo, spinning top, conkers, marbles, yo-yo, cigarette cards, pea shooter.

2. Housework

But what did women do all day at home? This box recalls those endless household chores.
Scrubbing brush, grate polish, cobbler's wax, pumice stone, Robin starch, washing tongs.

3. In The Kitchen

All sorts of kitchen tools and gadgets chosen to recall home cooking, baking and the art of making a little go a long, long way.
Tin opener, fly papers, pastry cutters, apron, bean slicer, whisk, candle, spills, recipes.

4. Going Shopping

Before there were supermarkets and a fridge in every kitchen, most housewives had to do the shopping every day and search for bargains to eke out the housekeeping money.
String bag, groceries, purse, old money, co-op tokens, butter hands, ration book, shopping list.

5. Looking Good

"We didn't have much, but we knew how to get done up like a dog's dinner in those days..."
Make-up, handbag, collars, studs, razor & razor strop, scarf, lace handkerchief, powder compact.

6. At the Seaside

Memories of outings, trips and holidays on the British riviera!
Sea shells, spade, seaweed, postcards, Brownie box camera, stick of rock, fishing line.

7. World War II - The Home Front

A selection of objects, pictures and documents recalling life in Britain during the War, and how people coped with the changes which War brought.
Newspapers, gas mask, ration book, ARP armband, identity card, blackout material, evacuee label.

8. Family Health

Recalling the days before the NHS began, when preventative medicine and hygiene were a family affair and minor ailments were treated with remedies from the home medicine chest.
Camphorated oil, zinc plasters, castor oil, nappies, chilblain cream, Thermogene wadding.

9. School Days

Brings back vivid memories of inky fingers and school dinners. The best days of our lives!
Smock, slate, chalk, pen & ink-well, ruler, pea-whistle, geometry set, belt, paper dart, satchel

10. Born in the Caribbean

Memories of home and social life, food, music and health remedies in the Caribbean islands.
Sugar cane, bay rum, country chocolate, dominoes, carbolic soap, herbs & spices, sarsaparilla, paraffin candles, traditional songs, map of the Caribbean Islands.